D0493623

2066 – and all that

Hugh
With good wishes,
courage.
Bill

2066 – and all that

BY
William Keegan

ILLUSTRATIONS BY

ιυγξ
iynx publishing

First published in Great Britain by
iynx publishing
Countess of Moray's House
Aberdour
Fife KY3 0SY

www.iynx.com

Copyright Text: © William Keegan 2000
Illustrations: © Wally Fawkes 2000

Trog acknowledges the help of Low, Vicky and Illingworth

The moral rights of the author and illustrator have been asserted

British Library Cataloguing-in-Publication Data
A catalogue record for this book is available from the British Library
ISBN 0-9535413-1-2

Text and cover design by Mark Blackadder

Printed and bound in Great Britain by Redwood Books Ltd, Bath

Acknowledgements

Among the people the author would like to thank for their comments on being subjected to a manuscript about EUROPE are: Jonathan Agnew; Ian Gilmour; Anthony Howard; Arnold Kemp; Alastair Macdonald; Hamish McRae; Adam Raphael; Lisanne Radice; Ray Richardson; Tom Short, Maurice Stonefrost and Geoffrey Wansell.

Thank you, also, to Teresa Goodman for bridging the channel between the author's 1966 typewriter and the demands of 2066 technology.

Contents

This book is dedicated to:
Clemency, Benedicta, Harry, Bartholomew (Lol),
Caitlin, James and Lucinda.

CHAPTER ONE

The Resumption of History

Britain's relationship with Europe began, as the authors of *1066 And All That* pointed out, in 55 BC. This was 'the first date in English History' when Julius Caesar 'the *memorable* Roman Emperor' landed at Thanet.

History came to a full stop, according to Sellar & Yeatman, in 1918, when American intervention (begun as late as 1917) led to the defeat of the Germans in the First World War, and America emerged as 'top dog' after the Treaty of Versailles (1919). This was, declared Sellar & Yeatman (writing in 1930), 'the end of history' – a declaration which anticipated Mr Francis Fukuyama's similar pronouncement (*The End of History and the Last Man*, 1992) by over sixty years.

History may therefore be said to have ended twice during the twentieth century.

Chapter Two

Why History Resumed

The US felt it was such a 'top dog' after the First World War that it did not make peace with Germany until 1921. This was in spite of the fact that President Woodrow Wilson was the driving force behind the Treaty of Versailles (1919) and the League of Nations (1920).

Unfortunately Woodrow Wilson was less of a driving force in his own backyard, and the US Senate refused to ratify the Treaty of Versailles. This meant that the US could not join the League of Nations, on which Wilson was so keen. As a result, there was still a lot of history to take place in Europe after all. Germany decided to make the most of it.

The big theme of Versailles was 'Reparations'. This can mean 'repair' or 'compensation'. The distinction between these two meanings is vital. The majority view of the Allies[1]

1. 'Allies' – i.e. Us (not just the US), or you and me – or at least our parents or grandparents.

was that the Germans deserved to be punished heavily for a) causing and b) waging the First World War. The emphasis of 'reparations' was therefore on compensating the Allies, not repairing Germany. This was to have Untold Consequences – i.e. beyond count, but told the world over.

The Allies were capitalists – sometimes pronounced in left wing circles as caPITalists, to emphasise how greedy capitalists are. Because they were capitalists, their main interest was money. They demanded lots of money, which the Germans did not have. Then the Germans discovered that they could just print the stuff.

Unfortunately, this also meant that the Germans discovered *inflation* – too much money chasing too few goods, or too little of everything. 'They've discovered lots of other things, so we shouldn't begrudge them the discovery of inflation', observed one scholar at the time.

The discovery did not, however, do them much good. They soon found that, the more they printed of their own currency (marks, *not* Marx), the less it was worth in foreign currency (dollars, pounds, French francs, etc.). So they still had great difficulty in meeting the demands for reparations.

Anybody could see that this was going to lead to

trouble and the Second World War (1939–45). *Anybody* was called John Maynard Keynes, a mathematician turned economist, who, unlike most economists, could write like a dream. This meant that people could understand his words, although they did not necessarily act upon them. 'You mark [sic] my words' said J.M. Keynes, 'making excessive reparations for **one** war will lead, as sure as night follows day, to another.'

Unfortunately, nobody listened to *anybody*, which is more or less what you'd expect. People marked his words, but did not heed them. Germany suffered Weimar, or 'wheelbarrow' inflation and high – very high – unemployment.

It was called Weimar inflation because from 1919 to 1933 the German Government was known as the 'Weimar Republic'. You would naturally assume that this meant the Government was based in Weimar. You would be wrong. Weimar was simply the place where the ill-fated post World War One German constitution was drawn up in 1919. If you think it wasn't as good as the post-1945 constitution, you are right. (Incidentally, the phrase 'wheelbarrow inflation' is not primarily a reference to the rising price of wheelbarrows, although these were undoubtedly in great demand: wheelbarrows were needed to carry enough marks – *not* Marx – to pay for a loaf of bread.)

But we should not lose our thread, which is what happened to Lord Salisbury (British Prime Minister at the turn of the nineteenth and twentieth centuries), who once sat down when speaking (or not speaking) in the House of Commons declaring, 'I have lost my thread.'

We have not lost our thread, or at least not yet. The point is that Weimar inflation and very high unemployment produced the social conditions which gave an obscure Austrian his chance. Unfortunately, he took it.

Chapter Three
Adolf Hitler – An Obscure Austrian

The 'obscure Austrian' was Adolf Hitler, an unemployed water-colourist. Adolf Hitler made the brilliant discovery that one way to cure one's own unemployment problem was to get a job promising to cure unemployment for everyone else. He therefore made himself president of his own political party. This was how he did it: he joined the German Workers Party one year (1919) and renamed it the next. Suddenly it became the National Socialist (or Nazi) Party. To make sure he kept his job, Hitler had himself declared life-time president. (Hitler was a little man, from a little country: he craved security.)

This all rather went to his head, and he decided to carry on where Attila the Hun and Genghis Khan had left off (i.e. for younger readers, to try to rule the world).

But first he had to rule Germany. He thought he'd start with Bavaria, because that was where he happened to be at the time. Bavaria, being contiguous to Austria, was the obvious place for an unemployed Austrian water-colourist to start trying to rule the world. Hitler liked Bavaria; he enjoyed the beer cellars of Munich in particular: he found that drinking their contents gave him Dutch Courage (see 'Maastricht' below). The Bavarians had other ideas however (the Bavarians were sensible *then*), and imprisoned Hitler after his failed 'Munich Putsch' (1923).

Hitler did not like the prison cellars of Munich as much as the beer cellars. Imprisoning him was a mistake: it gave Hitler time to think, and sort out his ideas. Whereas curing unemployment was a Good Idea,[2] blaming the Jews for Germany's defeat in World War I and making plans to exterminate them before and during World War II wasn't. Come to think of it, planning World War II wasn't either. (The historian A.J.P. Taylor thought Hitler did not plan World War II, but just stumbled into it. If so, he – Hitler – should have been more careful. What we do know is that he did not plan World War I.)

It was at the beginning of the 1930s that the British missed the chance to conduct their own 'Munich Putsch'. A gentleman called Lord Howard de Walden, subsequently to become a senior steward of the jockey club, was driving down one of Munich's main roads and knocked Hitler over.

Alas, the future dictator was unharmed. Back in the car, de Walden's companion told him who the stranger was. 'Hitler has a party and talks a lot,' he explained. Lord de Walden subsequently met Hitler for ten minutes and apologised for the accident. On this occasion, too, Hitler escaped unharmed.

2.   The autobahns were good; the armaments were bad.

Chapter Four

Marx, Lenin and Stalin in One Chapter

Hitler was not stupid – at least, not yet. But he always knew that, given enough power, *anyone* could act really stupidly. In his early days, however, he realised that, in order to win power and behave like The Biggest Megalomaniac of the Century, he had to pretend for a while that he was a man with a 'sane solution'. He had noticed that people tend to call for sane solutions when they perceive a threat. He had also noticed that people like uniting against a threat. Fear of communism provided him with just that.

For this, Hitler was grateful to Marx, whose parentage was not to Hitler's liking (although German, Marx was also Jewish), but who had more or less invented communism singlehanded (Marx was helped by Friedrich Engels, but still got most of the credit).[3] Brussels was the scene of the crime for most of Marx's work on the *Communist Manifesto* (1848); but it is difficult to blame 'Europe' or 'Brussels Bureaucrats' for this, because the European Commission was not invented until over 100 years later, and Monsieur Jacques Delors was but a gleam in his great grandfather's eye.

Marx passed Communism on to Lenin – metaphorically speaking, of course: Lenin was only thirteen when Marx died and had neither met him nor (yet) heard of him. Lenin had problems making communism work. These problems wore him down, and he died in 1924 at the age of fifty-four. Marx had lived to sixty-four, but then for him Communism was all theory with a bit of *Kapital* thrown in. He is buried in Highgate Cemetery, London, opposite the British sociologist Herbert Spencer. Marx and Spencer achieved many things but forgot to found the well known chainstore. Spencer did remember to coin the phrase 'the survival of the fittest'. Charles Darwin pinched it from him but Spencer had the last laugh and outlived both of them.

Lenin's death left the field open for The Second Biggest Megalomaniac of the Century, a former seminarian

3.   Life's like that.

named Joseph Stalin. It may reasonably be said that communism was bad for Lenin's health.

The Germans feared Stalin, though not half as much as the Russians did. They were worried by the spread of subversive communist movements to Germany itself. Since Marx had started inventing communism in Germany, and moved on to perfect his theory in Brussels, Paris and the British Museum (there you are: we're forgetting Engels already . . .), this just goes to show how subversive ideas get around.

What with Weimar inflation, high unemployment and fear of communism, things were falling into place for a once obscure and unemployed Austrian water-colourist to capitalise on people's fears. That's how Marx, Lenin and Stalin assisted Hitler's election campaign. The Nazis were democratically elected as the largest single party in the Reichstag in 1932. After that, it was a cake-walk for Hitler to manoeuvre himself into being offered the chancellorship of Germany in 1933.

Hitler celebrated his election victory by painting the town red. Unfortunately he went on to paint Europe red as well.

Chapter Five
Enter France

One of the recurring features of recent history had been the way Germany kept wanting to 'enter France'. Britain had entered France from time to time in the old days – not just because the British ruling class wished to secure its supplies of claret. The real British motive was to pay France, especially Normandy, back for 1066 (And All That). After the success of Henry V and various other plays, Britain had subsequently learned to stop entering France, and to 'become insular' instead.

'Becoming insular' meant concentrating on building an empire around the world rather than acquiring possessions in the neighbourhood of Calais or Château Pichon Longueville. True, Napoleon disturbed the peace a bit; but 'these things happen' (attributed to Josephine, who knew Napoleon quite well). This led to some nifty footwork by Wellington in the Peninsular War (1808–14), and by

Nelson at Trafalgar (1805) and other nineteenth-century last resorts. (It was Nelson who invented the non-telescopic lens.)

Napoleon had had a better time invading Austria (this was before Hitler's time) and Germany (often known as Prussia in those days) than Britain had invading France, and the Germans never forgave him for it, even though the Prussian General Blucher had helped Wellington to defeat Napoleon at Waterloo (1815). The Germans decided to get their own back by entering France in 1870, and again in 1914 (in fact it was Prussia that 'entered France' in 1870, and, flushed with this success, decided to be the leader of the New German Empire).

France was by now fed-up with 'being entered'. Wouldn't you be? After all, Napoleon had been dead for some time. France's perfectly understandable anger contributed to the heavy demands for reparations from Germany embodied in the Treaty of Versailles. (If you think this treaty has come up before, you have certainly been paying attention.)

Alas! As we have already noted, the reparations issue was a great help to Hitler, who decided in 1940 that it was a long time since Germany had entered France (a quarter of a century) and it was time to do so again.

Clemenceau (French prime minister during the Versailles Conference) had warned that the Treaty of Versailles did not secure France's borders with Germany. He was right.

Chapter Six

The Second World War (1939–45)

The First World War (1914–18) had been the War that will end War, and had led, briefly, to 'the end of history'. History resumed pretty fast (history tends to) and led to the Second World War.

The Second World War occurred once Hitler had achieved his ambition to become The Biggest Megalomaniac of the Century, with total control of Germany.

Enough is never enough, as Hitler had noticed during his deprived childhood. He now yearned for *lebensraum* ('more room for Germany' or 'space' as a more modern generation would have it). Under the Austrian (1526–1867) and Austro-Hungarian (1867–1918) Empires Hitler's native Austria had had lots of *lebensraum*. But some subjects felt they had more *lebensraum* than others, and the assassination of the Archduke Ferdinand of Austria by restless Serbs in Sarajevo had precipitated the First World War.[4]

Austria became a smaller country after the 1914–18 war; few scholars seem to have made the connection between Hitler's desire for *lebensraum* and the psychological impact of Versailles on the imperialist dreams of Austrian water-colourists.[5]

At all events, Hitler achieved *lebensraum* for a time. He achieved it by 'entering lots of other countries' – not just France, but Czechoslovakia, Poland and – well, any other country he could think of really. He didn't 'enter France' first, but that only fooled the Appeasers. Hitler even invaded Russia, having earlier signed a pact not to do so. This meant he was 'fighting on too many fronts,' and bound to be brought down in the end. That's the trouble with megalomaniacs – they fight on too many fronts. But that's not the only trouble.

Unfortunately, Hitler was able to carry out many of his nastiest designs before being brought down. These have been well documented. Our attention must now turn to the obvious question which raised its head after the 1939–45 war was over: how to stop the Germans doing it all over again.

4.   This was bad luck on Archduke Ferdinand, who had favoured the development of nationalist cultures within the Empire. But it was also bad luck on quite a lot of other people.
5.   Hitler himself made the connection in *Mein Kampf* but most scholars thought he was joking. Some joke . . .

Blank page to give reader a break, following research findings that the most popular saying in America after it came to the rescue of Europe in two world wars was: 'Give Us A Break, Chum.' (It wasn't just the fighting. Americans *over here* got fed up with being asked 'Got Any Gum, Chum?')

Chapter Seven

The Aftermath of the Second World War

The alert reader will be congratulating him or herself on his or her brilliant anticipation of the next point. If there was one thing the Allies knew they must *not* do in the aftermath of the Second World War, it was: make reparations the big theme of the post-war settlement.

It was not just *anybody* who knew that: by now *everybody* knew that. Indeed, the necessity to 'avoid another Hitler' was so impressed upon the subconscious of the Allies that, when asked 'What do you know?' (in the way one might ask 'How are you?'

or 'How's it going?') the average Ally would spontaneously reply, 'I know that we must not ask the Germans for too many reparations.'

Chapter Eight

The Aftermath of the Aftermath

Not asking the Germans for too many reparations was all very well. But what else to do? The Allies did what you, I, he, she, it or they would have done in the circumstances: they scratched their heads and had meetings. They scratched their heads and had meetings in Tehran, at Yalta and at Potsdam.[6] But they didn't just do this (scratch their heads and have meetings) in *these* places. They did so all over the place. For the great thing about big meetings is they have to *be prepared*.

Any diplomatist will tell you that the outcome of the best meetings is decided before you get there. Apart from anything else, this means that the great leaders can have

Next..

---

6.   You may well ask why they did this *in* Tehran but *at* Yalta and Potsdam. We don't know. It just sounds right.

more time to enjoy their meetings, slap one another on the back and pose for photographs for the history books (which these days means posing for that night's prime-time television).

It was Stalin who said to Churchill at Yalta: 'If you're going to make history, you might as well enjoy it,' to which Churchill ('ever the sage' according to his butler) replied, 'And if you're not going to make history, you still might as well enjoy it.'[7]

The thing the great leaders enjoyed most of all was being called 'The Big Three' (be honest, wouldn't you enjoy it?). In fact there were Five, because Roosevelt was succeeded by Truman before they had finished scratching their heads and having meetings, and Churchill by Attlee. Roosevelt scratched his head in Tehran, and at Yalta, but died in office before Potsdam. Churchill lived long enough to have been able to conduct a Third World War had he felt like it, but was thrown out of office by the British electorate in 1945.

Churchill thought this was a bit steep – and a bit rough on a chap who had won a war. Attlee, who won the 1945 general election, and attended the Potsdam Conference, took a different view.[8]

---

7. All right. We'll come clean: we made this up: but who knows? A whole school of historians has made careers out of the 'it is easy to imagine' approach; and it is easy to imagine how Stalin and Churchill *might* have said this.

8. Atlee scratched his head twice at Potsdam. Once in order to solve the world's problems. The second time because he couldn't really believe he was there at all.

Chapter Nine
Tehran, Yalta and Potsdam: The Truth

Tehran was in 1943, and Yalta and Potsdam in 1945 (if you see what we mean: they are still there, of course . . .).

It should be obvious to the meanest intelligence that, since Tehran was in 1943, the conference was concerned principally with how to finish the war. Similarly, since Yalta took place when the war in Europe was all over bar the shouting (of which there was lots by this time), and Potsdam (July 1945) took place after VE Day, these were about what on earth to do *after* the war.

The meanest intelligence would be right in both instances, and the Big Three (or Four or Five), who were themselves men of no mean intelligence, knew that their job was to

turn up and 'make history', but preferably different history from the sort made by Hitler, who in their (and everybody else's) opinion should not have turned up in the twentieth century at all.

Yalta was a famous Black Sea resort in the Soviet Union,[9] so Stalin was playing on home ground. This may help to explain how the atmosphere was shaped for the division of Europe at Potsdam and after.

Russia was doing well in the war: Stalin was in a position to tell Roosevelt and Churchill that, if they wished to discuss the future, they must go to him.

9. It continued to be in the Soviet Union until the latter collapsed (in 1990), and stayed on the Black Sea after the collapse. Some things in this world are more permanent than others.

The Big Three agreed on unconditional surrender for Germany, but argued about Stalin's proposal to 'dismember' the country. Churchill feared that dismembering or abolishing Germany, would leave a power vacuum at the very heart of Europe (this was a long time before John Major promised to put *Britain* 'at the very heart of Europe').

Churchill was almost certainly right. In the end the leaders partitioned Germany. The postwar occupation of Germany by the US, USSR, UK and *France* meant that there was (or were) now a Big Four.

It being a well-established fact that 'two's company but three's a crowd', it should have been obvious to *anyone* that Germany could not remain divided indefinitely into four parts. Why, even Caesar's Gaul had only had three! The stage was now set for the division of Germany into East and West.

Chapter Ten
Tehran, Yalta and Potsdam: More Truth

Potsdam was in what was shortly to be known as East Germany, which meant that Stalin was playing on home ground yet again. The Big Three discussed the political, economic and industrial future of Germany. They could not possibly have known what this was (or *would be*); but they were in a position to influence it. They decided to have a go.

One of the main objects of the postwar settlement was to stop Germany 'entering France' *again*. In some ways this was a West European point of view (and American, because, as Truman almost certainly observed to himself over breakfast in Potsdam: 'Sooner or later, whenever Germany enters France, we get dragged in, and it's getting to be a little bothersome.')

But Stalin had a different angle on the subject.

Roughly translated, his position was: 'What you guys fail to appreciate is that we must stop Germany entering Russia too.' Subsequent historians have regarded this as a pretty specious excuse for the way the USSR decided to hold onto Eastern Europe and introduce the Iron Curtain to the world. But that's the way these things go.

Chapter Eleven
The Iron Curtain

Most people put up curtains, or hang them. (Well: a lot of men manage to dodge the task until they are cornered. But you know what we mean.) *Iron* curtains, however, are by definition heavy; even if they are only metaphorical, they conjure up a pretty weighty image.

Stalin's way of not being entered by Germany again involved grabbing Bulgaria, Romania, Hungary, Poland, Czechoslovakia and a fair chunk of Germany itself.[10] You may well say his motives were imperial as well as defensive. You are at liberty to say anything you like, provided you don't demand your money back (we haven't got it; we've already spent it).

After much deliberation – we even had a meeting – we have decided that the only way to handle this problem (we are not trying to be ironical) is to say that Stalin *erected* an Iron Curtain. Churchill's actual words were: 'From Stettin in the Baltic to Trieste in the Adriatic an iron curtain has *descended* across the Continent.' But we stand by our belief that curtains do not simply appear from out of the blue, whatever Churchill may have said. This is perhaps also a good moment to show awareness that the phrase 'iron curtain' had been used by others before, including Dr Goebbels, to describe the Soviet sphere of influence. But timing is all, and Churchill gets the credit for using it at Fulton, Missouri, on 5 March 1946, when everybody noticed.

Which brings us to a small insight: the Cold War was to the Iron Curtain what steel is to iron ore; what a horse used to be to a carriage; and what Sinatra was to 'High Society'. Put simply: you couldn't have one without the other.

---

10. Stalin was like that.

Chapter Twelve

That Damned Curtain Again

Readers in outer space, formidable eyesight though they must possess, will no doubt be a little puzzled by now. 'You say the Allies went to war to protect Poland and save Czechoslovakia, so how come Poland and Czechoslovakia end up behind the Iron Curtain?' To which we say, as we have seen (or heard) done on television, 'Good question from that person in the back row.' Now, the conversational ploy 'good question' is most often used a) when one hasn't the faintest clue about the answer and needs to play for time, or b) when one has been practising a particular answer for days, has it off pat, and wants to make it sound even more dazzling by implying how difficult (and totally unexpected) the question is. Stalin and Hitler, to name but two Megalomaniacs of the Century, were adept at planting

people in the audience to ask good questions.

What the questioner from outer space is unaware of is that the Allies did *not* go to war with Germany in 1939: Britain did. The Americans did not get there until December 1941 (that Atlantic is quite wide even if it looks like a pond from outer space), when Germany went to war with them; moreover, Russia was actually on Germany's side until 1941 – or at least not against her.

Hitler's declaration of war on America came as a great relief to those who feared US isolationism would prevent President Roosevelt from coming to Europe's rescue. When asked, after the war, why Hitler had done this, the former Nazi foreign minister von Ribbentrop said Germany had been bound by its treaty with Japan and Italy. An interpreter interrupted: 'Why was that particular treaty the first one you decided to keep?'

When Hitler decided to fight on too many fronts, however, entering Russia fitted in neatly with his megalomaniacal tendencies.

For, in order to defeat Hitler, Britain had needed Allies. Stalin, or 'Uncle Joe' as he was affectionately known, had become an Ally in June 1941, feeling that Hitler's

invasion of Russia that month rather contravened the spirit of the Nazi–Soviet non-aggression pact of August 1939. (Hitler had thought, rightly, that invading Poland without coming to an arrangement with the Russians might upset Stalin, who had read his *Mein Kampf* and knew that Hitler had long term plans for *lebensraum* in Russia's direction. So they both invaded Poland, under the 'secret protocol' of their 1939 pact.)

At the end of the Second World War, Stalin decided to hang on to what he had got. The communist bloc managed to secure Poland, on whose behalf Britain had gone to war in the first place. Thus it was that Poland was liberated from the Greatest Megalomaniac of the Century, only to find itself in thrall to the Second Greatest Megalomaniac of the Century.

But the matter did not rest there. Just as France did not want to be entered by Germany ever again, neither did the USSR. Stalin's position as one of the allies who had helped to defeat Hitler put him in a strong position to bring Eastern Europe under his sphere of influence after the war. The communist coup in Czechoslovakia was not until 1948; but by then Stalin had consolidated his side of the Iron Curtain.

Which brings us to the big difference between the Two Greatest Megalomaniacs of the Twentieth Century. As Stalin remarked to the British Foreign Secretary, Anthony Eden, on their first meeting in 1941 (the beginning of the period when, having invaded Russia, Hitler made Stalin into our Ally), 'Hitler's weakness is that he does not know when to stop.'[11] Stalin did; he stopped at the Iron Curtain, and traded Greece for Rumania with Churchill.

Chapter Thirteen
The Cold War

In addition to being a great war leader, Churchill was also an outstanding orator, with a good turn of phrase. People with a good turn of phrase do not like to waste their efforts. There is evidence that Churchill worked hard on his good phrases – using them not now and again, but again and again. 'The same words will go down like a lead balloon one day, and be greeted as a good turn of phrase the next,' observed Churchill's friend Lord Beaverbrook.[12] 'You just have to keep on saying what you have to say' (North American for 'Repeat it').

Revisionist historians maintain that Churchill was not such a great war leader as all that. Revisionist historians are nearly always wrong – why didn't they get it right in the first place? Revisionist historians can be as bad as the 'butcheress' in *Remembrance of Things Past*. She couldn't get it

---

11. This is *not* one of the quotes we have made up.

12. At least, if he didn't, he should have done. Why have him as an adviser otherwise?

out of her head that the British, as well as the Prussians, had entered France in 1870.

His good turn of phrase helped Churchill to be a great war leader. When told to fight the Germans on the beaches, people tended to remember. When promised 'Blood, toil, tears and sweat', they remembered *that*, although not

necessarily in the right order, and usually omitting the 'toil', (We British are like that: see 'British Disease' below – not to be confused with *la vice anglaise* again, see below.)

Churchill maintained his reputation for a good turn of phrase after VE Day, as is demonstrated by the fact that it was he, not Dr Goebbels, who got the credit for coining the phrase 'Iron Curtain'.

Unfortunately, much as we should like to, we cannot credit Churchill with the phrase 'Cold War'. This was coined by Bernard Baruch, the US financier and man of parts. Among his parts was the co-ordination of American industry's war effort under President Wilson in the First World War. Another of his parts was working for President Roosevelt in the Second World War. Baruch really got around. He was working as an adviser to President Truman when he coined 'Cold War' in 1947, feeling he personally had had enough of hot wars.

Chapter Fourteen

The Minimum of Things You Need to Know about the Marshall Plan

Bernard Baruch, the man who coined the phrase 'Cold War', had worked on the economic aspects of the Treaty of Versailles. You may therefore deduce that he knew how to get things wrong.

Nobody wanted economic and political chaos in Western Europe after the Second World War – nobody in Western Europe or America, that is. But there is a theory, and some evidence, that the Russians did. As Stalin must undoubtedly have observed: 'Then we can extend our sphere of influence even further.' Many people thought Stalin had extended his sphere of influence quite enough by grabbing, among others, the countries for which Britain had gone to war, such as Poland – not to mention a few more on whose behalf we had not gone to war at the time, such as Czechoslovakia, Hungary, Rumania, Bulgaria and Yugoslavia (up to a point: Tito had resisted the Germans during the Second World War and resisted the Russians afterwards).

There was also the little matter of the way Moscow encouraged communist insurrection in Greece, and communist movements in France and Italy.

Things were pretty rough in Western Europe during the winter of 1946–47, and US official, William L. Clayton couldn't help noticing. After he reported back to Washington, General George Marshall, Secretary of State, said: 'The United States should do whatever it is able to assist in the return of normal political health in the world.' By this he meant: 'Weimar and Isolationism have had their day and didn't do too well. Europe needs dollars.'

Marshall had also been across the Atlantic and concluded 'the patient is sinking'. But the subsequent European Recovery Programme was the work principally of President Truman and Marshall's successor, Dean Acheson. It was nevertheless called the Marshall Plan. How come? Well, President Truman was so busy coining aphorisms such

as 'the buck stops here' and 'a week is a long time in politics' that he often didn't have time to leave the desk where the buck was stopping. So he got Acheson to make the preliminary speech on the European crisis and Marshall to unveil the idea of the plan.

It happened like this: Marshall went to Truman in the nearest the unflappable general could muster to a panic and said he (Marshall) had got to make a speech at Harvard. What was he going to say? Truman, being very altruistic, replied: 'I want you to spell out the details of this plan that's being worked out over in the State Department to save Europe from going under. This plan is going down in history as the Marshall Plan, and that's the way I want it.'

Since Marshall was in charge of the State Department at the time, it was helpful of Truman to remind the general of what was going on there, even if Marshall himself had ordered it. Churchill described the Marshall Plan as 'the most unsordid act in history'. Truman said: 'We were in a position to keep people from starving and help them preserve their freedom and build up their countries and that's what we did.'

Truman twisted strong arms in Congress to get the

money. Marshall won the Nobel Peace Prize for the plan. Truman said: 'It is amazing what you can accomplish if you do not care who gets the credit.'[13]

Dean Acheson, Marshall's successor as Secretary of State, observed: 'I have probably made as many speeches and answered as many questions about the Marshall Plan as any man alive . . . and what citizens and the representatives of Congress alike always wanted to learn in the last analysis[14] was how Marshall Aid operated to block the extension of Soviet power and the acceptance (by Europe) of Communist economic and political organisation and alignment.'

13. Apparently it was President Truman's idea, and Marshall took the credit. Truman didn't mind, as long as it was *done*. They don't come like that any more.

14. We have not, as yet, been able to establish whether Dean Acheson's use of the term 'in the last analysis' constituted the seminal moment when the phrase 'in the last analysis' became obligatory in serious discussion of anything. But we believe it preceded the term 'at the end of the day' by several decades; and, on balance, in the last analysis, we prefer it.

THE BUCK STOPS HERE

THE MARSHALL PLAN STARTS HERE

A Week is a Long Time in Politics

Chapter Fifteen

The Reconstruction of Western Europe

Anyone could see that Western Europe needed reconstructing after 1945. And one particular anyone was still around. John Maynard (now also 'Lord') Keynes, who had warned about the futility of Reparations, now devoted himself to the post-war economic order.

When negotiating with Morgenthau, the US Secretary to the Treasury, over how to ensure full employment, low inflation and other worthy objectives in the post-war world, Keynes noticed something. He could never command Morgenthau's full attention, because the great man was continually interrupted by telephone calls from Capitol Hill, during which Morgenthau would say 'Yes senator' and 'No senator.'

Now, the reader may say it is not difficult to notice such interruptions; but some people, notably such Megalomaniacs of the Century as Hitler and Stalin, enjoyed the sound of their own voices so much that they seldom noticed when they were being interrupted. Keynes was not a man to fail to notice when he was being interrupted. He therefore devised a stratagem. He said goodbye to Morgenthau and returned to his hotel. He telephoned Morgenthau from the hotel. 'And then', Keynes subsequently told friends, 'I finally found I was able to engage the Secretary of the Treasury's full attention.'

Thanks to these and other noble efforts by many *anybodies*, the process of reconstructing Western Europe and avoiding another Weimar began.

Chapter Sixteen

Tying Germany Down in Europe

In probably the most famous pronouncement on the subject during the twentieth century, Henry Ford declared: 'History is Bunk.'[15] This was not a reference to Bunk Johnson, the New Orleans jazz trumpeter; it was a reference to history. Sometimes things are what they seem – but not very often. As a manufacturer of motor cars, Henry Ford naturally felt he knew a lot about history.

No: the most interesting observation about history is that statesmen and politicians are always fighting the last war. 'Dead battles, like dead generals, hold the military mind in their dead grip and Germans, no less than other peoples, prepare for the last war.' Thus wrote Barbara W. Tuchman in *August 1914* – which was about the war that wasn't the last war.

15. In fact, he said 'History is more or less bunk.' He wasn't quite sure. But it doesn't sound so good like that.

The question arises, of the post-1945 settlement: were the leading statesmen and politicians also making the mistake of fighting the last war? *They* said: 'Of course not. Why, the whole point of the post-1945 settlement is that we shall *not* fight the last war – or the previous one, come to that.'

Whether or not you think they had got the point, everybody in the West was now faced with the question: how to tie Germany down in Europe? (a little late in the day, you might think), thereby curing her of her unfortunate habit of 'entering France' (and other places we could name).[16]

Now, what was the second question? Ah yes: how to prevent the Cold War from becoming another hot war.

Chapter Seventeen
The Founding Fathers

Reasonably reliable research has established that most Europeans have mothers. During the decade after 1945, however, the great bulk of European mothers were too busy keeping the bodies and souls of their families together to worry about higher issues. 'Looking after our own issue is quite enough,' declared a typical European mother.

Many women think men are a bit slow on the uptake (*c.f.* most feminist literature, *passim*). Be that as it may, even European men noticed that there were no founding mothers of Europe in evidence during the period 1945–55. 'This leaves a gap for us,' said a distinguished Frenchman called Jean Monnet[17] to distinguished Frenchman Robert Schuman. '*We* could be the founding fathers of Europe, and thereby make our contribution to History.' 'I agree,' replied

---

16. Of course, the problem might have been solved once and for all by tying Germany down in New Zealand. But nobody thought of that.

17. Not to be confused with Monet the great Impressionist. Jean Monnet was no oil painting but a great man nevertheless.

Monsieur Schuman – or, to be more precise, 'D'accord, Jean – after all, the United States had founding fathers, and we're older than they are.' 'Even if we don't behave like it,' said Monnet. And so the idea of a United Europe was born – or, at least, conceived.

Chapter Eighteen
The Founding Fathers – Part Two

Monnet had served as Deputy Secretary General of the League of Nations. He therefore felt he knew quite a lot about what a disunited Europe looked like. Schuman was Foreign Minister of France at the time of his historic conversation with Monnet, having, in common with many French statesmen after 1945, served as prime minister for a few months. It was entirely logical, for the foreign minister of a logical nation that did not want to be entered by Germany again, that Schuman should propose the Schuman Plan. What would *you* have done if your name was Schuman and you had reached the age of sixty without proposing a plan?

Monnet and Schuman had been taught at an early age that oaks grew from acorns. 'If we are going to tie Germany down in Europe then we have to start somewhere,' observed Monnet. There was a momentary pause, and then Monnet added the words his interlocutor had been waiting for: 'I know what. *I've* already *had* a plan.' (The Monnet Plan for French industrial modernisation, 1946.) Schuman waited with bated breath: 'So we'll call this the Schuman Plan.' Robert Schuman smiled seraphically, but then frowned: 'Oh dear, Jean,' he said. 'Does that mean I'll have to draft it? I'm quite busy, you know what with being Foreign Minister and so on.'

In addition to being someone of statesmanlike vision, M. Monnet was a kind man. He immediately put M. Schuman at his ease. 'Oh no, Robert, you don't have to worry about anything like that. *I'll* draft it for you.' Pause, 'You see, although I say it myself, I'm quite good at drafting plans. You might say I do it for a living.'

Chapter Nineteen
The Schuman Plan

Monnet and Schuman got very excited about the Schuman Plan. Wouldn't you, if *you* were intending to change the course of history? Why, even Henry Ford himself might have got excited, whether he believed in history or not.

'But what are we going to put into the Plan?' asked Schuman, after the effects of the aperitif, the burgundy and the armagnac had worn off. 'These things are more easily said than done.' There was a characteristically Gallic pause. 'In my experience,' replied Monnet wittily, 'these things are more easily done than said.'

Schuman looked puzzled. 'I am highly intelligent, Jean, and very well educated. Furthermore, I think what you have just said is extremely funny. But if you'll forgive me: I know I've had a lot to drink – what exactly does it mean?'

'I am surprised you take my little joke so seriously, Robert,' said M. Monnet with a twinkle in his eye. 'I was merely alluding to the fact that getting things agreed by governments and committees is, in my experience, extremely hard work.'

'Whereas *doing* them – implementing them – is comparatively easy? Ha, ha. I see. Very droll. Jean.'

Thus it was that Schuman and Monnet experienced one of those moments of communion in which true partnership is born.

Chapter Twenty

The Schuman Plan – The Vital Details

The alert reader will have remembered that Monnet and Schuman had been taught from an early age how oaks grow from acorns. It would not be too much of an exaggeration to say that their shared obsession with this truism altered the course of European history. One can arguably push the analogy between acorns and coal and steel a little too far. What the Schuman Plan proposed was a 'common market' – but a common market confined in the first instance to coal and steel, the production of which within France, Germany, Italy and the Benelux countries would be planned by a 'supra-national' organisation.

The European Coal and Steel Community was set up in 1952. 'This is the acorn from which the Treaty of Rome and the rest of the common market will grow later in

the decade,' Jean Monnet said prophetically to Robert
Schuman over a celebratory *armagnac*.

'It can hardly be denied', noted the Italian economist
Tommaso Padoa-Schioppa some forty years later 'that
establishing joint supra-national management of coal and
steel – the two fundamental natural resources of the
nineteenth and early twentieth centuries, over which France,
Germany and the rest of Europe fought cruel wars – was a
highly political project.'

'Stealth and bureaucracy – that's what done it,' said a
British official many years later.

Chapter Twenty-One
Coal, Steel and Bumps-a-Daisy

Coal and Steel; Steel and Coal: the European Coal and Steel Community. It all seemed harmless enough. But for the British Government it was political dynamite. When the ECSC was first mooted, Britain had a Labour government. Coal and Steel? These, to British socialists, were 'the commanding heights' of the economy. (Not to be confused with North Sea oil, discovered some decades later, and more like the commanding depths.)

At about this time, the Labour Cabinet Minister Herbert Morrison was discovered in a smart London restaurant in an emotional state, sighing 'The Durham miners won't wear it.' Police enquiries subsequently established that the influential Morrison was referring not to reluctance on the part of the Durham miners to wear iron, steel, nylons or any other form of apparel, but to their (presumed) refusal to be part of a European 'supra-national' organisation.

'Why,' said the leader of the Durham miners 'after all these years of being ground down by the coal-owners (pronounced 'cool-owners'), we've just won a great (pronounced 'greet') victory.'

He was not referring to the Second World War, but to the nationalisation (pronounced 'nationaliseyshun') of the pits. 'We're not going to throw that away, Geordie Lad,' said the leader of the Durham miners to the leader of the Northumberland miners. And a Labour government was not going to hand over newly nationalised industries to 'foreigners'.

So that was that.

Chapter Twenty-Two

For Empire and America

Or was it? (Note for readers with short memories: this is a reference to the last sentence of the previous chapter.)

It was not just the miners and the Labour Party. It was most of the Establishment. The 'Establishment' was a term popularised by the political journalist Henry Fairlie, in The *Spectator*. The Establishment[18] was worried about the Commonwealth – if not the Empire. And there was the 'special relationship'.

'Let's face it,' said our establishment man at the Foreign Office, 'a large proportion of the map is coloured Imperial Red. And, quite frankly old boy, *we* like it and that's

18. The word 'Establishment' dates from 1481 – Brewer says: 'A term long used to denote in particular the established Church of England, but now a popular designation for the influential hierarchy or inner circle in any particular sphere of the community, *or of the community in general* [our italics]. It has a somewhat derogatory significance associated with reaction, privilege and lack of imagination.'

how *they* like it. I could go further,' he said, and continued before anyone could stop him. 'These Benelux countries, and – which other country is it? Italy? – these other countries may tag along with the Coal and Steel Community, but we have our Commonwealth and our "special relationship". Errm, that is to say: we have – had – an empire, which is becoming a Commonwealth; and we *have* a special relationship with the United States – why, not so very long ago we won a war with them – that is to say: not *against* them, but on their side – once they had come in, that is – took them a bit of time, what?'

At this stage, true students of history do not need to be reminded of the Monroe Doctrine; but we shall remind them just in case. You never know these days what people pick up in history lessons, what with all these large classes successive governments have promised to do something about.

The Monroe Doctrine had nothing to do with the film star Marilyn Monroe – just as Nelson's Column in Trafalgar Square has nothing to do with Nelson Mandela. James Monroe was the Secretary of State and President of the United States who proclaimed in 1823, 'Hands Off

America': European powers were not to intervene in the Americas (North, South or in-between) and, *quid pro quo* or dollar for dollar, the US would not intervene in Europe.

In fact, once again we are reminded what a cheat history can be, even if we do not go as far as Henry Ford in describing it as bunk.[19] For, you've guessed it, just as the Schuman Plan was largely the work of Jean Monnet, so the Monroe Doctrine was largely the work, not of the Monroe family, but of John Quincy Adams. John Quincy Adams was something of a hero because he was also against slavery – although by all accounts a slave to his work.

19. More or less.

Chapter Twenty-Three

Britain and the Common Market

'Right from the start, Europe was a political act.' When making this assertion, British observers refer not to Europe, but to EUROPE. Britain has been part of Europe for as long as anyone can remember. But it is was an open question whether, even in the 1990s, it was part of EUROPE.

EUROPE was an alien place with which many people, especially Conservative members of Parliament, knew we had become involved but would rather we had not. Britain was in favour of EUROPE getting its act – or Act – together, provided we did not have to be involved ourselves. Why: the whole point of EUROPE's getting its act (or Act) together was so that we need not be active on the Continent of Europe (or EUROPE) again – involved, that is, in the aftermath of Germany 'entering France' yet again.

Notwithstanding the Monroe Doctrine, the US had actively engaged in European affairs twice within twenty-five years – and at our (we Europeans') behest.

Which brings us to the Acheson Doctrine, for which the present authors claim exclusive rights, because it has not been enunciated in quite this way before – or so we fondly imagine. Dean Acheson, US Secretary of State, famously declared that 'Great Britain has lost an empire and has not

yet found a role.' It was tacitly understood that, in making this declaration, Acheson was not for one moment suggesting a reversal or an adulteration of the Monroe Doctrine, and that the UK should somehow rediscover a role in North America – say in Boston Harbour or Saratoga, or even Quebec.[20]

No: Dean Acheson meant that Britain had failed to find its role in EUROPE. Why? Because it was concentrating on its special relationship with America. And what was the special aspect the US wanted to emphasise? Britain's place in EUROPE . . .

Ah, well. You win some and you lose some.

20. Rediscovering a role in Quebec would have been particularly poignant. As everybody educated in a small class knows, James Wolfe said he would prefer to have written Gray's 'Elegy' than to take Quebec. This has prompted some scholars to observe that if Waterloo was won on the playing-fields of Eton, Quebec was taken in a country churchyard down the road. Wolfe didn't write Gray's 'Elegy' – and he died while taking Quebec.

Chapter Twenty-Four
Roles and Relationships

In his memoirs Dean Acheson describes Britain's failure to join the European Economic Community from its inception as 'one of the greatest mistakes of the post-war era'.

In 1940 Churchill had proposed an 'indissoluble union' between Britain and France. By 1946, however, he was in favour of a United States of Europe, that did not include Britain. Britain's policy then became one of 'encouraging the others.' Unfortunately, the British Government decided, some years later, that by encouraging the others it had discouraged, indeed disadvantaged itself.

During the late 1950s and early 1960s the standard reply in British Establishment circles to 'What do you know?' or 'What's happening?' became 'Those wretched Europeans are drawing ahead of us', or 'Those French seem to plan things better than we do.'

Now, it is a well-established fact that, after a time,

people become fed-up with standard replies to standard questions and need a little variety.

During the 1940s and early 1950s the British had plenty of variety, in the form of variety shows and the good old British music hall.

As the decade of the 1950s progressed, however, the British became dissatisfied with their own variety. The decline of the British music hall became a recurring theme, and, although he later became a folk-hero, Archie Rice in John Osborne's *The Entertainer* was taken to represent the tired state of Britain, its music hall and its variety.

Meanwhile, the Empire was collapsing, and Britain was having problems with the transition from Empire (including the Kingston Empire) to Commonwealth (the 'Kingston Commonwealth' was not even tried as a business venture in England, and would have been taken to refer to something in Jamaica).

Harold Macmillan might have declared that 'the wind of change' was 'blowing through this continent' [Africa] in 1960. In fact the gales of change had been much in evidence since the Second World War, with the British army fighting rearguard imperial actions in Malaya, Kenya, Cyprus and one or two other areas they had won as consolation prizes for the Boston Tea Party.

So, one day the answer to the questions 'What do you know?' and 'What's happening?' included not only 'Those wretched Europeans are drawing ahead of us' and 'The French seem to plan these things better than we do', but also 'We've lost the Empire too.'

Now the alert reader – or readers, if you like doing these things in groups – will be saying, 'Ah, yes, that's all very well, but what about the "special relationship"? Wasn't that some kind of consolation prize?' To which, unfortunately, the Garter Keeper of the Royal Consolation Prizes had the answer as long ago as 1956. 1956? Does that ring a bell? Yes, 1956 was the year of Suez and Hungary, the year in which – hang on a minute: can we be dreaming this? – Britain found itself having a 'special relationship' with France in a joint action to reclaim the Suez Canal from Colonel Nasser – an Egyptian – who had noticed one day that the Suez Canal stopped at Suez; that Suez was in Egypt; and that he was the undisputed ruler of Egypt.

Chapter Twenty-Five
North of Suez

In the film of *Gone with the Wind* Rhett Butler, or Clarke Gable as he was more commonly known, said he 'couldn't give a damn'. In 1956 the US Government decided it could not give a dam to Egypt.

President Nasser retaliated by nationalising the Suez Canal Company.[21] Israel invaded Egypt, and a joint Anglo-French expeditionary force was despatched 'to separate the combatants'. Since these were combatants Britain and France had done their damnedest (as it were) to join together, Britain and France got into the finals of the 'most disingenuous diplomatic explanation of the year' competition.

For some extraordinary reason, the Anglo-French force landed a lot nearer to the canal than to the front line. That's the way these things go sometimes.

---

21. All right, it was slightly more complicated than that. Nasser had been asserting himself for some time. But what a coincidence!

They acted in collusion with the Israelis, although this was denied at the time. The phrase 'to separate the combatants' was used by Sir Anthony Eden, now the British prime minister. It was to Eden, it will be recalled, that Stalin had made his great remark: 'Hitler's weakness is that he does not know when to stop.'

Eden's weakness was that he did not know that Colonel Nasser was not Adolf Hitler. But Eden did know when to stop. He stopped when the Americans told him to.

The Americans did not like this show of neo-imperialism on the part of the British and the French. They were worried that the Russians might jump in and heat up the Cold War.[22]

The problem for Britain was that Uncle Sam held the purse-strings. When the pound was in trouble the US Treasury usually propped it up. Britain's revival of nineteenth-century gunboat diplomacy at Suez terrified the world's financial markets as much as it frightened the natives. The pound took a dive; the US refused to prop it up.

The Suez adventure was over. Delusions of imperial grandeur were shattered. Britain's 'special relationship' with

22.   They did – but not in Egypt. The Russians just invaded Hungary instead.

the US did not look in too good a shape either.

One of his ministerial colleagues who had urged Eden on was Harold Macmillan, the chancellor of the exchequer. One of the colleagues who told him he had to stop, because the Americans wouldn't wear it, was – well, Harold Macmillan. And the man who succeeded Eden as prime minister after the Suez affair had broken him was – no – it would be unfair to ram home the point.

Chapter Twenty-Six
Special Relationship

Suez was not just a canal: it was also a watershed. Not only was Britain's relationship with the world never going to be quite the same again: Britain's relationship with itself was in trouble. The country was divided *for* and *against* 'Suez', just as it was at odds every year over the annual battles between Oxford and Cambridge on another great waterway, the River Thames.

'Suez' allowed Russian tanks to 'enter Hungary' and suppress the contemporaneous uprising. This was not funny.

The 'special relationship' between Britain and France over Suez, or *Entente Encore Cordiale*, was short-lived. Despite the evidence of history (and geography), Britain continued to pursue the Holy Grail of a 'special relationship' with the US, under the premiership of Harold Macmillan (1957–63). That is to say, Macmillan was Prime Minister of Britain during those years, not of the US, although Macmillan had delusions of grandeur, being particularly fond of dukes, grouse moors, 'special relationships' and, well, grandeur.

What Macmillan did have was a special American relation – his mother. He also treated another American as a kind of adopted nephew. The young man was called John Fitzgerald Kennedy.

During Kennedy's prominent, but brief (1961–1963), presidency much was made of the avuncular relationship between Macmillan and Kennedy – particularly by the 'uncle'. Blue Streak, Skybolt – various missiles were developed with American assistance, so that Britain could retain its great power status with an 'independent' nuclear deterrent.[23]

For Macmillan (now known as 'Supermac') and Kennedy (now known as JFK), Britain could be Athens to America's Rome. Well, for Macmillan, anyway.

Kennedy, or JFK, did not become president until five years after the Suez affair. He might have been more inclined to help Britain out at Suez. Just imagine that . . .

On second thoughts, don't dare to imagine that. For it is time to turn our imagination to something that *was*

23.   Independent of everyone except the Americans, that is.

happening, although Britain would have preferred that it *wasn't* happening. We refer of course to the beginnings of EUROPE (not Europe, which had been around since Julius Caesar, or at least since 1066).

In order to understand EUROPE we have to try to understand Charles de Gaulle. Many have tried, but few of them have been English.

Chapter Twenty-Seven
Charles de Gaulle – the Man, not the Airport

After the fall of France in 1940, General Charles de Gaulle sought refuge in London from the Petainist French government which collaborated with the Germans. De Gaulle took exception to the way the Germans had 'entered France' yet again. Unlike Caesar the Germans took the view that Gaul should be divided into two parts. De Gaulle especially disliked this 'Veni, vidi, Vichy' approach.

De Gaulle saw himself, in Groucho Marx terms, as the party of the third part. He became Leader of the Free French, of whom, it has to be said, there were not many. De Gaulle was irked by the sad condition of France, and by his relative impotence as leader of the Free French in London.

Although considered an honoured guest by the British Government, de Gaulle sometimes got above himself, which was quite difficult, since he was 6' 7".[24] The best known focus of the activities of the Free French in London, while pleasurable, was of limited strategic value, namely the York Minster public house, in Dean Street, Soho.

Above all, de Gaulle was humiliated by his, and France's, dependence on the US and Britain for the removal of all those Germans who had 'entered France'. (When we say 'his' and 'France's' dependence, we wish to avoid the confusion sometimes generated by the expression, commonly attributed by cartoonists to de Gaulle in later years: *'La France: c'est Moi.'*)

There are people in life who react badly to charity and to assistance of any kind. De Gaulle, while he liked to consider himself unique,[25] was just one of many in this respect. After America had helped Britain to win the war, and enabled him personally to re-enter France, de Gaulle spent much of the rest of his life spurning the US and the UK.[26]

---

24. Authors' estimate. The great man was so tall, nobody could reach all the way up there with a tape measure. Anyway, they would have measured him in metres.
25. He *was*.
26. People are like that.

Towards the end of the war, de Gaulle left London to become head of the Committee of National Liberation in Algiers (1943). After France had been liberated, de Gaulle put in a timely appearance in the streets of Paris and was made president of the 1945–46 provisional government.

The general disappeared from the French political scene in 1946, retiring to Colombey-les-Deux-Eglises. He was recalled to deal with the Algerian crisis of 1958 – on the principle that retreats are best conducted by strong men – and made President of the Fifth Republic in 1959. (Most countries have only one republic but France does everything to excess.)

Please remember these dates: they mean that de Gaulle was around at certain times and not at others. That's how history happens.

Chapter Twenty-Eight
Macmillan and de Gaulle – The Odd Couple

Charles de Gaulle, future President of France, and Harold Macmillan, future Prime Minister of Britain, were in North Africa at the same time in 1943. They once went swimming together. Or, rather, they didn't: Macmillan stripped off his clothes and swam from the rocks; de Gaulle sat, fully clothed in uniform, and watched him.

Macmillan did not get into difficulties, so on this occasion de Gaulle did not have to decide whether to let him sink or swim. Of course, it may simply have been that de Gaulle could not swim anyway. At all events, the abiding impression was of the general's stand-offish[27] approach to Macmillan's great venture into the sea – a portent, if ever there was one, to subsequent Anglo-French relations. For de

27. Or 'sit-offish'. The General was sitting on the rocks at the time.

Gaulle had indubitably shown his hand: indeed, this was about the only part of his anatomy he did show. There are no pictures of General de Gaulle jogging.

Macmillan should have been forewarned. When his bid to join what was then the 'Common Market' was made in 1963; when Macmillan put his toe in the deep waters of the *English Channel*, manfully faced France and said '*S'il vous plait, Monsieur le Président, moi et ma tante veulent beaucoup joindre le Marché Commun,*' de Gaulle replied: '*Non, Monsieur, vous avez manqué le bateau.*'

Chapter Twenty-Nine

Britain in Dire Straits – Long Before the Pop Group

Thus in 1963 Britain's European policy was on the rocks. As foreign secretary in 1955 Macmillan had been one of the majority of the British Establishment who were deaf to the 'European' overtures from across the channel.

With that deft touch for the reading of European history for which Whitehall has become renowned, a British civil servant, Russell Bretherton, attended the Messina Conference (1955), which led to the Treaty of Rome (1957) and proclaimed: 'The future treaty you are discussing has no chance of being agreed; if it was agreed, it would have no chance of being ratified; and if it were ratified, it would have no chance of being applied. And if it was applied, it would be totally unacceptable to Britain. You speak of agriculture, which we don't like, of power over customs, which we take exception to, and institutions, which frighten us.'[28]

After this *tour de* weakness Mr Bretherton is said to have concluded: '*Monsieur le president, messieurs au revoir et bonne chance.*'

The president whom Mr Bretherton addressed was not de Gaulle but Jean Monnet, founding father of the High Authority, the precursor of the European Commission.

Monnet always wanted Britain *in* EUROPE. But while he may have been the founding father of EUROPE, he was not Mr, or *Monsieur*, Big.

Monsieur Big (still estimated at 6' 7") was Charles de Gaulle. In 1955, and indeed in 1957, when the Treaty of Rome was signed, de Gaulle was *not around*: he was *between* presidencies; between *les deux églises*; and in no position to prevent Britain from joining EUROPE.

But from 1958 to 1969 de Gaulle *was* around. What was more, he was around as President of France, in which capacity he saw one of his occasional duties as being to veto

28.   Mr Bretherton was of course referring to institutions which begin at Calais.

any British application to join EUROPE that might come along.

While de Gaulle was around, Britain's relations with EUROPE were in dire straits. For a generation of British 'pro-Europeans', Messina was the rock on which the good ship *Britain in Europe* foundered. The Straits of Messina, of course, are popularly supposed to be where Scylla and Charybdis hung out in the old days.

Chapter Thirty
The Three Harolds

Although Britain had lost its empire, it was just about hanging on to the Rolls. The country took the successive 'Nons' from General de Gaulle with a stiff upper lip.

When saying 'Non' to Harold Macmillan in 1963, de Gaulle accused his wartime hosts of being 'insular and maritime'. This was a little unfair because if they hadn't been insular and maritime, they might have been entered by Germany in 1940 and unable to protect their wartime guest. There is no gratitude in these matters.

When saying 'Non' to Harold Wilson in 1967, de Gaulle said Britain would have to make 'very vast and deep changes'.

It was not clear whether this meant removing the English Channel. What was quite clear was that de Gaulle still did not want to go swimming with anyone British.[29]

29. The Channel itself has never been very clear. The pollution started with Julius Caesar's first crossing.

William the Conqueror had defeated King Harold at the Battle of Hastings in 1066; Charles de Gaulle defeated the two modern Harolds – Macmillan and Wilson – in 1963 and 1967 with magisterial pronouncements from the Elysée Palace.

This was one – or perhaps two – in the eye for Harold M. and Harold W. But the first Harold had really got it in the eye. The reader may think it is difficult to associate King Harold directly with the failure of the EEC negotiations 900 years later, but can be assured that PhD students, desperate for originality, are working on it – on *both* sides of the Channel.

Chapter Thirty-One

Monsieur Pompier Au Secours – or President Pompidou to the Rescue

1968 was the year that Europe's students revolted against the 'affluent society', thereby demonstrating that you can have too much of a good thing. This was to lead to the revival of the economic doctrine that affluence should go principally to those who are affluent already. After all, the latter know how to enjoy it.

In 1968 the wine was bad but the riots were good. For an entire generation 1968 means 'riots in Paris'. Now, *somebody* had to negotiate with the revolting students of Paris. No, that somebody was not John Maynard Keynes (long deceased); it was the French statesman, Georges Pompidou.

Georges Pompidou had negotiated a settlement for de Gaulle with the revolting Algerians in 1962. By comparison, negotiating a settlement with the revolting students of Paris in 1968 was child's play, or 'jouer avec les enfants'.

Pompidou had served under de Gaulle during the Second World War, and had been his personal assistant in 1958–59, helping, among other things, to draft the new French constitution. This was quite an achievement, because France had given the impression of requiring a new prime minister every fortnight, and having no time for new constitutions.

De Gaulle had failed with the revolting Paris students in 1968 and Pompidou had succeeded. What better man to take on the revolting British and handle their feeble attempt to join the rest of Europe?

Britain was now able to capitalise on the fact that de Gaulle was no longer around at a time when she *did* want to join.

In Georges Pompidou, Britain could not have picked a better 'non-vetoer' if she had conducted the French presidential election herself.

Chapter Thirty-Two
Britain Joins Something

Despite, or because of, his long apprenticeship to de Gaulle, Georges Pompidou took a different view from his mentor of Britain's role in Europe. He believed Britain's history and geography placed her firmly in EUROPE. Pompidou could read maps as well as history books. (De Gaulle didn't need to.) For Pompidou Britain's adventures with 'empire' were but minor aberrations from her traditional close links with Julius Caesar, the Vikings, William the Conqueror, Bordeaux, the Spanish Armada, the Napoleonic Wars, and two twentieth-century world wars that began in EUROPE.

Monnet might have started the European Economic Community to stop Germany from 'entering France' again; but there was physical 'entry' and political 'entry'. Pompidou saw Britain, if she really wanted to join, as a counterweight to Germany in peace as well as in war.

If de Gaulle and Macmillan had not got on as

swimming partners, Pompidou and Harold Wilson did not hit it off as dining companions. Indeed, Wilson, on one important occasion, failed to come to Pompidou's table at all. This was in July 1966, when Pompidou visited London as French prime minister, and Wilson withdrew, at short notice, from a dinner engagement.

The pretext could hardly have been more offensive to Pompidou, who concluded that Wilson was not serious about EUROPE. The pretext was that Wilson had to attend a House of Commons debate on Vietnam. For Pompidou, trying to be more understanding than de Gaulle about Britain's obsession with the world stage and its special relationship with the US, this was 'unfortunate.'

If Wilson had, as he expected, won the 1970 election, the relationship between him and Pompidou would have been unlikely to prosper. But the new prime minister, Edward Heath, was a Europhile if ever there was one. He spent two whole days convincing Pompidou of his good intentions, omitting only the flowers and the ring.

Pompidou pronounced: 'The spirit of our talks over the last few days enables me to think that the negotiations will be successful.' The French president also gave a passable impersonation of Edward G. Robinson saying: 'Don't bother me with the details.'[30]

30.   Accent on second syllable of 'details'.

Chapter Thirty-Three

A Very British Referendum

President Pompidou had left the boring details of the trade negotiations surrounding Britain's entry to the EEC to officials. The history of EUROPE was not to be held up by haggling over butter, sugar and meat – or not yet. Britain's entry on 1 January 1973 was a triumph for Edward Heath.

But it's tough at the top of Europe, as all the European leaders featuring in this saga – Hitler, Stalin, etc. – would have testified had they still been around. The lustre of Edward Heath's success in the Elysée Campaign was tarnished by a spot of bother at home. The spot was inflation and the bother was a miners' wage claim.

When Heath called an election early in 1974 on the issue 'Who Governs the Country – the prime minister or the miners?' – the answer was: not the prime minister – or, at

least, not *this* one.

Just as Wilson was astonished to lose the general election of 1970 (he was way ahead in the opinion polls), he was amazed to win the general election of February 1974 (when Labour were behind in the polls).

Wilson was a pragmatist: the man whose European credentials Pompidou distrusted had no desire to disentangle Britain from the EEC. But the party he led was dominated by its insular left wing.

Wilson felt it expedient to bow to left-wing demands for the Common Market issue to be 'put to the people' in a referendum. Being a conservative nation, Britain voted for the *status quo*. As the country was already in the Common Market, people were reluctant to step out into the cold. They voted to stay in the heat (not Heath) of the Brussels kitchen by a handsome margin of two to one. If there had been a referendum about entering EUROPE in 1972–73, the British people might well have voted to stay out. The art of Conservative leadership is to know when not to be conservative. Edward Heath had *not* had a referendum about going in.[31]

31. He just *did* it.

Chapter Thirty-Four
Meanwhile, Back in the World

Meanwhile, back in the world, the post-Hitler settlement was in trouble. The Americans had done the decent thing, and stayed in Europe, rather than retreat into isolationism. But they had mistaken a communist assault on South Vietnam for a communist invasion of the world (see 'domino theory').

The abortive attempt to save South Vietnam from communism cost money. The almighty dollar was rocked. The oil producers of the Middle East (and elsewhere) did not like being paid in devalued dollars. They decided to flex their muscles.

It was not easy to see Arab sheikhs flexing their muscles from this distance. It was easier to see what was happening to the price of oil (or 'gas', depending on which side of the 'special relationship' you stood).

By the time the price of oil (or gas) had quintupled, it was easier to see Arab sheikhs too: they were all over London's West End, buying it (the West End that is, not oil – they were *selling* that).

The world was becoming a rougher place. European leaders took several looks at one another and decided: 'We need stability.'

Chapter Thirty-Five

Schmidt, Giscard, Callaghan and Jenkins – the Twelve Tone Quartet

Helmut Schmidt was Chancellor of West Germany from 1974 to 1982. Valéry Giscard d'Estaing was President of France from 1974 to 1981. This meant that Schmidt and Giscard kept bumping into each other.

They kept bumping into each other at the regular meetings of the European Economic Community that resulted from the founding fathers' desire that Germany should never 'enter France' again.

It was all right for individual Germans to enter France; Schmidt did so may times in the course of his duties. Likewise his friend, Giscard, entered Germany from time to time. Whenever, and wherever, they met they conversed in English.

On one occasion the two leaders harked back euphorically to the glories of Charlemagne and the Holy Roman Empire, under which parts of Germany and parts of France had been bound together for hundreds (and hundreds) of years. They did so at a meeting in Aachen (or Aix-la-Chapelle – you see what we mean). This was a good place to celebrate closer ties between France and Germany, since it had been Charlemagne's northern capital in the good old days and entered by both France and Prussia over the years.

Giscard and Schmidt were worried about 'money'. Most people are worried about money, but great statesmen worry about *big* money – the dollar, the mark, the franc – that sort of money. With a statesmanlike leap of the imagination, Schmidt also connected his worries about big money with his worries that Jimmy Carter (President of the United States from 1977 to 1981) was a weak president.

It was but a logical next step for Schmidt and Giscard to call for a zone of monetary stability in Europe.

On such occasions it helps to have an ally. Their ally turned out to be British politician, Roy Jenkins, who was President of the European Commission from 1977 to 1981.

Jenkins decided to make an important speech, capitalising on the general mood. So in 1977 he went to Florence and reminded everybody of the founding fathers' ultimate aim of EUROPE (not Europe). Schmidt, Giscard and Jenkins were the political driving forces behind the formation of the European Monetary System (EMS), or Exchange Rate Mechanism (ERM), as it became more widely known.[32]

But the curse of de Gaulle lingered on: Callaghan did not put the British pound into the ERM at its inception in 1979 because the Labour Party, still predominantly anti-EEC, would not wear it.

Schmidt and Callaghan got on well personally. They had a meeting in Bonn in 1978 at which the main topic on the agenda was whether or not Britain would join the ERM. An expectant Europe waited. When the two came to address the press afterwards, they talked about the situation in Namibia.

32. In Dublin the initials EMS stood for 'Easy Money Soon'.

Chapter Thirty-Six

Mrs Thatcher's Bread Crisis

During the early years of her government, Mrs Thatcher presided over a doubling of the inflation and unemployment rates. Since she had promised to reduce both, she became 'very unpopular'. The overvaluation of the pound, in particular, made large sections of British industry uncompetitive.

But Mrs Thatcher had either read, or been told about, *Henry IV – Part One*. She decided to 'busy giddy minds with foreign quarrels' – not just in the Falklands War but also earlier on in the war of Britain's rebate from the EEC.

Mrs Thatcher thought EUROPE was *unfortunate*. She also thought the Foreign Office was *unfortunate*. The Foreign Office had forecast that Britain would alter the rules of the

EEC once she[33] joined. This showed serious ignorance of the fundamental principle of the EEC: 'First come, first served.' The 'rules of the club' had not been fashioned in Britain's interest. But the 'Iron Lady' went on the rampage in Europe, demanding changes in the formula by which Britain's contribution to stopping Germany 'entering France' was calculated. When offered some concessions, she was not satisfied and asked for more. She declared that she was not prepared to settle for 'a third of a loaf'.

After she had got nowhere, her foreign secretary, Lord Carrington, and his deputy, Sir Ian Gilmour, successfully negotiated 'two thirds of a loaf'. It was obvious to *anyone* that this was the best possible deal available. Mrs Thatcher told them she would resign rather than accept it. After many hours they realised she was more interested in a continuing row with EUROPE than in reaching a settlement.

Undaunted, Carrington and Gilmour briefed the press that it was *her* achievement. Once faced with an exuberant tabloid press, Mrs Thatcher graciously accepted her triumph and declared the bread crisis over.

33. 'She': Britain, not Mrs Thatcher. Mrs Thatcher never joined EUROPE.

Chapter Thirty-Seven
Thatcher, Kohl, Mitterrand – Resistance and Collaboration

President François Mitterrand, elected in 1981, decided that Mrs Thatcher had 'the lips of Marilyn Monroe and the eyes of Caligula'. Chancellor Helmut Kohl of West Germany cut off a discussion with her in Salzburg on the pretext that he had an urgent appointment; a few minutes later she went out into the street and discovered that Kohl's appointment was with himself: he was at a pavement cafe tucking into a large cake. It is not known whether Mrs Thatcher asked for two thirds or the whole cake.

Kohl and Mitterrand got on well. Mitterrand's wartime career had been devoted to collaboration *with* and

resistance *to* the Germans. Thatcher got on well with President Reagan. It is not true that she said 'that is because he speaks my language'. But the two had a rapport. She encouraged Reagan to 'up the stakes' against 'the Evil Empire', while the French and German leaders were more cautious. The latter, after all, were nearer to what they hoped would not be the action. Meanwhile, though 'talking tough', the Iron Lady cut the growth of Britain's defence spending.

While Mrs Thatcher and President Reagan were dancing to each other's tune, nothing much was happening in Europe. In the absence of anything better to do, the European commission, under its president, Jacques Delors, decided it was time for another push towards ever closer union.

The EEC might have removed most of its internal tariff barriers, and might act 'as one' when it came to trade negotiations with the rest of the world. But there were still many 'non-tariff' barriers within the EEC: these were known as the French, the Germans, the British and various other groups. For some extraordinary reason, people had a habit of favouring their fellow countrymen in awarding contracts, and were absolutely devoted to their own particular form of electric plug.

The time had come, said the Brussels bureaucrats in the mid-1980s, for all the barriers to come down and to make the whole of the EEC into a 'single market'. They chose 1992 for the target date, for no better reason than that it was *not* there – at least, not yet. Some signatories to the big proposal thought 1992 would never come. And, by the way, '1992' was to begin in 1993.

Although Mrs Thatcher thought EUROPE was *unfortunate*, she seized upon the Single Market as a way of exporting 'Thatcherism' to EUROPE. The winds of competitive change would enable the newly resurgent Britannia to sweep through Europe. British companies were leaner and fitter as a result – well, as a result of Thatcherism.

Unfortunately, if bureaucrats have nothing better to do, they dream up schemes for expanding their empires. Why not, they asked in Brussels, have a single *currency* as well as a single market?

Technical Annexe for connoisseurs of, or contracting parties to, technical details about certain aspects of recent, but seemingly distant, monetary history.

There is nothing new under the European sun. The Romans introduced a single currency in Europe, but it declined and fell (*see* Gibbon, entreaty of). After a brief interval, European heads of government met at the Hague in 1969 and decided there had been too many currency fluctuations since the collapse of the *denarius*. They looked around for someone who had enough time on his hands and their eyes alighted on Pierre Werner, prime minister of Luxembourg (pop. 392, 000). M. Werner was instructed to draw up the Werner Report, examining the possibility of introducing economic and monetary union by 1980 – which would mean a single currency.

M. Werner duly reported in 1970, but the possibility remained a possibility. The idea was that, as a first step, EEC countries would tie their currencies more closely together – even more closely than they were tied to the dollar under the Bretton Woods exchange rate system. Unfortunately the EEC governments chose pretty well the worst time possible to do this: currency markets were in turbulence, and the Bretton Woods system was in the process of breaking down, thanks to the inflationary pressures on the dollar, the linchpin of the system. (*see* Vietnam War, inflationary financing of and, Bad Timing, limitations imposed by . . .)

The EEC currency arrangement was called 'the snake'. Don't ask us why, but it certainly poisoned the atmosphere. Within two months of the birth of the snake, the German Deutschmark made an excuse and left. Undaunted, the EEC had another go in March 1972. With Britain on the verge of joining the Community (which it did on 1 May 1973) the pound was put into the 'snake' on 1 May (moving day) 1972; it stayed there precisely seven weeks and four days. This was *not very long*. Sterling's ignominious departure from the snake was not a *sterling performance* (or perhaps it was, depending on whether you were a Eurosceptic.)[34]

The experience was to influence the British Establishment's attitude towards European currency arrangements for a *long time* and possibly until 2066. Even

the French franc left the snake, in January 1974. In a gesture worthy of De Gaulle himself, the French put the franc back into the snake in 1975, but again it could not stand the strain, and departed after a few months. There weren't many currencies left in the snake, which proceeded to cast its skin into the Deutschmark bloc.

It suited all concerned to forget that the Werner Committee had proposed in 1970 that EUROPE should have a 'single' (or 'community', as they called it) currency by 1980. Be honest: do *you* remember the Werner Committee – even if you were on it?

And it suited the British Establishment to conclude that, thenceforth, all European currency arrangements would come to no good.

34.   At the time, the term 'Eurosceptic' was but a gleam in the *Daily Telegraph's* eye.

Chapter Thirty-Eight

Mrs Thatcher Becomes A Singular European

When Mrs Thatcher signed the Single European Act in 1986, she thought she was beginning the Thatcherisation of Europe. But the small print stated that there would be an increase in the powers of the European Parliament, and that the logical next step to follow the single market was European economic and monetary union (EMU).

By this very act, Mrs Thatcher was transformed from politician into a statesman. She demonstrated that she had lost her eye for detail. This was a woman who prided herself, until then, on reading so many details that she only took four hours sleep a night.

The Foreign Office attempted to reassure her: 'Don't worry Prime Minister. It will never happen. EMU is just one of those things these Europeans feel they have to aspire to.

Remember the Werner Report?'

'The What?!'

Mrs Thatcher might have been fêted on the world stage as the Iron Lady, but she felt increasingly beleaguered on the home front. And when she discovered that her chancellor of the exchequer, Nigel Lawson, was secretly conducting a policy under which the pound was 'shadowing' the German mark, she was furious.

One of her advisers said at the time: 'Mrs Thatcher does not like the Germans. Her views on Germany were *set in stone* in 1944.'

Worse was to come.[35] European leaders had asked their central bankers to draw up a blueprint of what economic and monetary union would look like *should* they (the leaders) decide to go ahead with it.

Mrs Thatcher had personally chosen Mr Robin Leigh-Pemberton as Governor of the Bank of England. She hoped he would sabotage the 'Delors' Report on EMU. He was, after all, Lord Lieutenant of Kent.

But Mr Leigh-Pemberton 'went native' and became *very* EUROPEAN.

35. It tends to.

Chapter Thirty-Nine
Collaboration and Resistance – the Wall Falls Down

R.L. Stevenson had said it was better to travel hopefully than to arrive. The European Economic Community (EEC), which became the European Community (EC) in 1987, had been founded on twin hopes: that EUROPE would prevent Germany from 'entering France' again; and that a United Europe would be better able to face up to what Mrs Thatcher's friend, Ronald Reagan, was to term 'the Evil Empire'.

But when the Berlin Wall came down in 1989, neither Mrs Thatcher nor President Mitterrand liked what they saw. Both were unhappy about the reunification of Germany: this might have been a goal towards which the former Allies had been travelling hopefully for forty-four

years – US Secretary of State, James Byrnes, had proclaimed this goal in 1946; but, as far as Mitterrand and Thatcher were concerned, it was a unified Germany that had caused all the trouble in the first place. A unified Germany was never quite meant to arrive.

The logic was: an unemployed Austrian water-colourist had caused trouble in a unified Germany; if Germany were reunited, then – who knew? – a latter day unemployed Austrian water-colourist might again cause trouble. He would be unlikely to be called Hitler, because Hitler sired no offspring to anyone's knowledge, and most people called Hitler had changed their name by deed poll to innocent-sounding substitutes such as Haider.

Despite her passionate diatribes against communism, Mrs Thatcher had been quite happy with the *status quo* in East Germany. She had been especially happy with a World Bank study in the late 1970s which suggested that East Germany's living standards had overtaken those of the UK. This was convenient propaganda against the Labour government she was about to displace.

But when the Wall eventually came down, and West Germans made a proper inspection of their eastern cousins' territory, what they found was, in the words of one Bonn official: 'An Economic Junk-heap'. This meant that unification was going to cost a lot.

The problem was simple. As our man in Bonn explained: 'If West Germany does not put a lot of money into East Germany, then a newly-freed East Germany will put a lot of people into West Germany.'

It was an historic moment. It was not every year that post-war chancellors had the opportunity to reunite Germany: politely though Helmut Kohl listened to Mrs Thatcher and President Mitterrand, his attitude was 'Let me eat cake'.

Helmut Kohl did what *anybody* would have done in his (quite large) shoes. He ignored Thatcher and Mitterrand.

Helmut Kohl seized the historic moment and opted for economic and monetary union between west and east Germany. He told his fellow (West) Germans before the 1990 elections that this would not involve higher taxes.

Helmut Kohl lied to unite his country.

Chapter Forty
A Small Town in Holland

Having collaborated with, *and* resisted Germany during the wartime occupation, and having done the same with his political colleagues ever since, President Mitterrand was put out of his stride only momentarily by the reunification of Germany.

Mitterrand decided to redouble the efforts France had made, via the Delors Report, to pursue European economic and monetary union. 'It is now imperative that Germany be *tied down* in EUROPE,' said the French élite.

Chancellor Kohl agreed. Kohl belonged to the generation that did not trust Germany to behave itself. This was because Kohl's generation had seen Germany not behaving itself. Indeed, some members of Kohl's generation – but we had better not go into all that again . . .

The Delors committee had conveniently produced a blueprint for European economic and monetary union, should heads of government wish it.

After much discussion, seemingly endless negotiation, but only minor revisions to the blueprint, European heads of government agreed The Treaty on European Union at Maastricht in December 1991. The Treaty was formally signed in the same small town on 7 February 1992 by the high contracting parties. To confirm that true statesmen do not like to bother themselves with the details, the British chancellor of the exchequer, Kenneth Clarke, admitted he had not read the treaty.

The blueprint was adopted by Britain up to a point. Mrs Thatcher had been removed from office in 1990 by her own colleagues, not least for her hostility towards EUROPE. The Conservative Party showed itself as predominantly hostile to EUROPE only after her demise.[36] Thatcher's successor, John Major, could only approve the Treaty of Maastricht, and steer it through the House of Commons, after negotiating clauses keeping Britain's options open.

John Major had said he wanted to be 'at the very heart of Europe'. He spent several days there. Thatcher had been removed for being anti-EUROPE. Major could only

36.   That's the way these things go.

survive by being anti-EUROPE.

President Mitterrand's master-stroke was to insist with Chancellor Kohl that a firm deadline be put on the process of tying Germany down in Europe. The so-called 'single' currency was to be introduced by 1999 at the latest. That way France would finally make its mark (not *Mark*) and the Germans would lose theirs.

Chapter Forty-One

Maastricht

Hitler had wanted *lebensraum*, or space. Helmut Kohl and François Mitterrand remembered Hitler. A whole generation of French technocrats was determined that European economic and monetary union would so tie Germany and France together that another war between the two countries would be unthinkable.

French economic policy had for some years been geared to making the French economy fit to be bound more closely to the German economy. If sexual flagellation had been considered by the French to be *la vice anglaise*, economic flagellation, or sado-monetarism, was considered by British observers to be *la vice française*.[37] France, whatever happened to unemployment, was determined to prove that it could achieve German inflation rates in perpetuity.

37. British observer's ought to know: Mrs Thatcher had invented 'sado-monetarism'.

The greater part of the motivation behind the move to a 'single' European currency was thus political. There were also those French technocrats who argued that a single European central bank would be a means of putting 'French fingers in the Bundesbank till'. The argument was that monetary policy under the control of a European central bank would be more 'accommodating' than the way the Bundesbank effectively controlled European economic policy at the time.

But the Bundesbank only controlled other countries' monetary policies if those other countries let it. (Britain's monetary policy was under the control of the Bundesbank while the pound was in the European exchange rate mechanism between 1990 and 1992, but not afterwards.) And the Bundesbank was not stupid. It had insisted, during the Delors and Maastricht deliberations, that the statutes of the proposed European Central Bank (ECB) should be at least as tough as its own and that there should be strict limits on what governments could spend.

A senior Bundesbanker said: 'Surely the politicians won't be mad enough to adopt these conditions.'

The politicians adopted the conditions at a small town in Holland.

Chapter Forty-Two

No More Wars in Europe

Something else happened at Maastricht. In return for being understanding with the British about their 'opt outs', and with the French about the 1999 deadline for EMU, the Germans got the others to bow to pressure for the recognition of an independent Croatia.

Croatia was part of Yugoslavia. Its recognition as an independent state was a factor – only a factor; we put it no higher than that – in what followed: the first war within Europe since Hitler. A Tito-less Yugoslavia was bound to fall apart some time.

Oh, and by the way: the Croats, the Serbs, Bosnians – all shared a single currency.

Chapter Forty-Three

A German Europe or a European Germany?

Neither Mrs Thatcher nor Mr Major liked the idea of a single European currency. Nor did they warm to Brussels, to 'federalism', or to the dilution of British 'sovereignty'. In the heyday of the British Empire we had ruled the waves while trying to maintain the balance of power in Europe. Now we spend all our time Waiving the Rules. Every September the Empire is celebrated, as if it still existed, at 'The Last Night of the Proms' – in a concert hall named after Queen Victoria's German husband. The Last Night includes a rousing rendition of 'Land of Hope and Glory', with the emphasis on 'wider, still and wider'.

    Width has always appealed to the British.[38] After the

38. Hence the old East End comment on the Empire: 'Never mind the
    quality – feel the width . . .'

Fall of the Berlin Wall, the British ploy was that Europe should concentrate on 'widening' rather than 'deepening'.

'Widening' meant putting the emphasis on expanding what was, after Maastricht, called the European Union, to include former members of the Soviet Bloc, such as Poland, Hungary and the Czech Republic. 'Deepening' meant Maastricht and the Single Currency.

For Chancellor Kohl, the importance of tying Germany down in Europe meant 'widening' *and* 'deepening'. This had nothing to do with the fact that Chancellor Kohl was wide and deep himself.

Chapter Forty-Four

Federalism for Beginners – or Utterly United

During the debates about whether Europe should deepen or widen or both, two things became crystal clear in Britain: the split on Europe within the ruling Conservative Party was deepening, and support for the Conservative Party was not widening.[39]

Mrs Thatcher had wreaked revenge on the 'Europhiles', such as Chancellor Nigel Lawson, Foreign Secretary Sir Geoffrey Howe and Heir of All Seasons, Michael Heseltine, who had contributed to her downfall. Under her leadership the Conservative Party in the country had moved so far to the right that the newer intake of Conservative MPs, especially in the 1992 general election,

---

39. An all too rare example of British understatement. Please treasure.

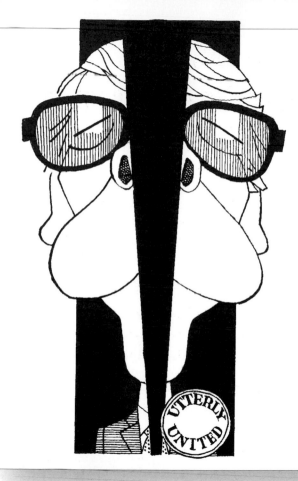

UTTERLY UNITED

were Thatcherites without their cause: *She* had been elevated to another place.[40]

Now, on the rapidly burgeoning Conservative Right, there were fears of plumbing the twin depths: loss of political sovereignty to 'Brussels' – which was blamed for all ills, including the unpopularity of any 'directives' from Brussels which had been insisted upon by the British Government itself; and domination by Germany.

To the Germans, 'federalism' means the diffusion of political power. To the Conservative Right, it meant 'the concentration of political power'. This kind of confusion doesn't half make for interesting debate.

An infamous cover of the right wing *Spectator* magazine depicted Chancellor Kohl as a modern Hitler, hell-bent on German domination of Europe. This was somewhat at odds with Chancellor Kohl's mission to ensure that there were no modern Hitlers *ever*, and that Germany should *not* dominate Europe.[41]

As the splits within the Conservative Party deepened further, the British Prime Minister described his cabinet

40. Which is what the House of Commons calls the House of Lords – and Ladies too.
41. In Britain we believe in a free press – free to write any old rubbish.

team as 'utterly united'. This was a strange use of 'utterly' – normally a pejorative term – and an eccentric interpretation of the meaning of 'united'.

Chapter Forty-Five

Chunnel Time or Britain Joins Europe – Official

Whereas the debate about Britain edging closer to EUROPE has been a relatively recent affair, the question of linking Britain and France by tunnel has been around for nearly 200 years.

It is to the discredit of Caesar, Julius, and Normandy, William of, that neither thought of a tunnel, or 'Chunnel', as a way of bringing EUROPE closer together. Napoleon's thoughts about a Chunnel were naturally viewed with suspicion in London, as was the brief attempt at a Chunnel in the early 1880s.

Another false start was made in the early 1970s, and the Chunnel finally got moving, as it were, in 1987, to be completed in 1994.

Thus the Chunnel was constructed during the

Thatcher/Major years, and the prevailing philosophy prevailed, as prevailing philosophies have a habit of doing. Mrs Thatcher insisted that, at least on the English side of the Channel, recourse should not be had to public finance in the construction of the Chunnel. The prevailing philosophy stated, unequivocally: 'The private sector is good; the public sector is bad.' This view triumphed over everything, including the fact that, as prime minister, Mrs Thatcher herself worked for the public sector, and received her salary and accommodation from public funds.

At one stage the British prime minister was even against the idea of the Chunnel. She changed her mind after being plied with scotch whisky at the British Embassy in Paris. There are diplomatic sources who believe the Chunnel was only built because the British Prime Minister had had 'one over the eight'. Our lawyers tell us that such suggestions can be dismissed out of hand.

The French had no scruples about injecting public funds into the project.[42] But commercial banks had great

42. Nor did socialist President Mitterand have any scruples about injecting French public funds into Chancellor Kohl's right-of-centre Christian Democrat party to help it stay in power. Mitterand and Kohl were prepared to buy their way to the single currency and, what's more, they did it with other people's money.

CHUNNEL VISION

difficulty in financing the Chunnel without British government help. Nobody wept for the banks. Despite teething troubles, the Chunnel was 'A great success' – for those who didn't invest in it.

But old habits died hard. The British people still talked about 'crossing' the Channel, not 'going under' it. This is because the British have spent 1000 years of history not going under.

Chapter Forty-Six
A Government Falls

It was not enough to construct the Chunnel to bring Britain closer to EUROPE (metaphorically speaking, of course: EUROPE remained twenty-one miles away). Britain also needed a change of government.

Mr Major's declaration that he intended to put Britain 'at the very heart of Europe' remained an intention. Mrs Thatcher might have been removed from office by fellow ministers partly because of her 'anti-Europeanism'. But she had the last laugh. The Conservative Party she reluctantly bequeathed to Mr Major was so anti-European that Major was eventually drowned in a tide of Euroscepticism.

Their Euroscepticism was not the only reason why the Conservatives lost the general election of 1 May 1997. The Conservatives lost the election because the British public said: 'We have had enough.'

But the fight between the Europhiles and Eurosceptics made the Conservative Party look utterly disunited. This was because they *were* utterly disunited.

Chapter Forty-Seven

Britannia Waives the Rules

Europe hoped that, after resoundingly winning the general election of 1 May 1997, Mr Tony Blair (known in EUROPE as 'Toni Blayr') would abandon all scepticism and sign up for the single currency.

Within months of his victory, Mr Blair was clearly thinking to himself: 'If leading Britain is so easy, I need a new challenge. I shall try to lead EUROPE as well.'[43]

For a few weeks in the autumn of 1997 there seemed a possibility that Britain would abandon all scepticism and sign up for the single currency. Such thoughts were encouraged by a report in the *Financial Times*.

But New Labour, as they styled themselves, were nervous. Mr Blair discovered that, even with a 93 per cent

43. Leading Britain is not so easy. *We* know that. Mr Blair had yet to find out.

personal approval rating in the opinion polls, he could not walk on water, nor even on the English Channel. Opinion polls also showed that two thirds of the British people were *against* the single currency.

Other things being equal, the opinion polls would not have mattered to a strong leader such as 'Toni Blayr', with a 180 majority in Parliament. But other things were not equal. Labour had been nervous in opposition, and in its election manifesto had committed itself to a referendum on the single currency, should Cabinet and Parliament decide to join during the next, i.e. 1997–2001 (or 2002), parliament.

To scotch rumours that an early decision was imminent, the chancellor of the exchequer, Mr Gordon Brown, unveiled 'the five economic tests' (27 October 1997). These would have to be satisfied before the government would contemplate joining 'a successful single currency'. The tests covered 'the effect on investment, the impact on our financial services industry' and 'whether it is good for employment'. (That's three of them.) They also included 'whether there is sufficient flexibility to cope with economic change' (on both sides of the Channel). That made four. Far the most important one was 'whether there can be sustainable convergence between Britain and the economies of a single currency'.

The convergence test related above all to whether the same interest rate would suit EUROPE *and* the UK. Since UK interest rates at the time were double those of EUROPE, it was generally thought that 'convergence' would take some time, and hardly occur during the 1997–2001 (or 2002) parliament.

'These tests' said an anonymous Treasury official 'are as long as a piece of string'.

Strictly speaking, the referendum 'pledge' related to the 1997–2001 (or 2002) parliament. But the government felt bound to adhere to this commitment if re-elected. Meanwhile the Euro-sceptic opposition Conservative Party, under William Hague, was trying to make hostility towards the single currency into a major (not Major) election issue.

The British people had voted to stay in Europe in 1975. Would they vote to take a leap into EUROPE shortly after AD2000? Or would they wait until, say, 1000 years of history had elapsed since 1066, and opt for 2066?

In a speech on EUROPE in July 1999 Mr Blair departed from his script. 'To be in, or not to be in,' he said. 'that is the question.'

CHAPTER FORTY-EIGHT

To Be In, Or Not To Be In . . .

The next chapter will contain an examination paper. To assist readers who have got this far to take the final leap (or running jump as it is known in less polite circles), the following extracts from two relevant articles are provided free of charge:

(i) **Treaty Establishing the European Economic Community, Rome 1957**
Article Two: 'The Community shall have as its task, by establishing a common market and progressively approximating the economic policies of Member States . . .'

(ii) **Treaty on European Union, Maastricht 1992**
Article Two (Replacing Article Two of the Rome Treaty): 'The Community shall have as its task, by establishing a common market and an economic and monetary union . . .'

Candidates are advised to abstain from sex and violence during the examination which follows.

Chapter Forty-NINE

A Nation Decides

Write on one side of the Channel only.

All questions should be attempted.

A French or German translation is not required.

Part One
MULTIPLE CHOICE

Tick the statement which in your opinion most captures the spirit of Britain's relations with 'Europe':

(a)   Well, yes and no.

(b)   On the one hand . . . and on the other.

(c)   *Je ne sais pas*

(50 marks)

Part Two
MULTIPLE CHOICE

The then Liberal Democrat Leader, Paddy Ashdown, said, after a 'warm' speech delivered by Tony Blair about the euro, that the prime minister had:

☐   'Crossed the Rubicon'

☐   'Put his toe in the Rubicon'

☐   'Put his foot in the Rubicon'

(50,000 lire for the correct answer)

Part Three
ESSAY

William of Normandy came for a day trip in 1066 and stayed. If 1000 years of history are to be honoured, does 2066 seem the appropriate year for Britain to invade the euro? State your reasons clearly, from the viewpoint of a Europhile *and* a Europhobe.   (150 francs)

Part Four
ESSAY

What does the future hold?

(As many euros as you can fit into your pocket)

CHAPTER FIFTY

From Now On, You're On Your Own